Get Outside
MAKE A NATURE
SCULPTURE

EMILY KINGTON

HUNGRY
TOMATO™

CONTENTS

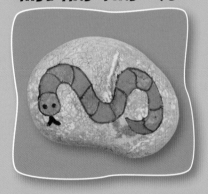

NATURE SCULPTURE

Going outside is lots of fun, and we can get crafty at the same time. Here are eight things to make from stuff that you can easily find when you are outside.

Get your rain boots on and go on a scavenger hunt. Turn the page to see what things you need to find . . .

HELPFUL TOOLS

Gloves

Rain boots

Old bag to carry items home

Small trowel or old spoon

Scissors

You will need a grown-up to help make these fun nature projects!

SCAVENGER HUNT

You need to find...

Moss

Dig it up from the forest floor. It's best if it has a little dirt.

Bark

Look for loose bark. Don't peel it off trees—they need it!

Vines

Vine stems can be used to tie things together.

Leaves

Find dry leaves of all shapes and sizes.

Stones and Pebbles

Look for different shapes, sizes, and colors.

Sticks

Always be on the lookout for sticks of all different sizes.

Wood

Collect interesting pieces of wood.

Seeds and Cones

Pine cones, acorns, and seeds will look great on your projects.

Mud

The stickier the better. You could also use paper clay.

LONG-NECK DINOSAUR

Find some old bark to make this cool dinosaur!

YOU WILL NEED

Good-sized piece
  of mud
Old dry bark
Sticks
Acrylic paint
Super glue

1 Push four sticks into the piece of mud to make the legs.

2 Break bark into pieces for the tail, body, and head.

3 Paint eyes on the head. Paint a small piece of bark red and glue it to the head to make a mouth.

4 Glue the body to the top of the legs, and glue the tail and head to the body.

You can almost hear this dinosaur ROAR!

STICK MEN

Make a funny stick man or a whole group of stick men friends. Put the stick men in a pot or into a garden.

YOU WILL NEED

Small sticks
Moss
Seeds or acorn tops
Mud
Super glue
Acrylic paint
Paintbrush
Old plant pot (optional)

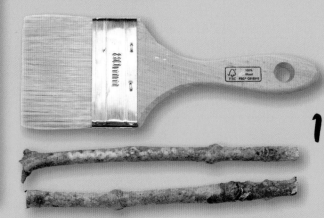

1 Clean the sticks by brushing them with a paintbrush.

2 Paint each stick different colors.

3 Add faces and hair using seeds, acorn tops, and moss.

4 If you are using a pot, fill it with mud and lay moss on top.

Add a big stone for them to stand around.

5 Put your stick friends in a pot or in a garden!

PEBBLE PEOPLE

You can make pictures using pebbles and stones.
It's easy for small hands to do too!

1 Wash your pebbles in soapy water and leave them to dry.

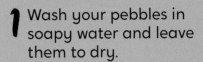

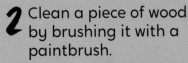

2 Clean a piece of wood by brushing it with a paintbrush.

3 Organize your stones to make people.

4 Spread mud onto the wood. It needs to be thick enough to push the stones into.

Here are some people watching the sun go down!

5 Push the stones into the mud. Add a nice round stone and some leaf stems for the sun!

SHIP AHOY!

You can make this pirate ship in no time at all. Add a pirate stick man who can sail it away!

YOU WILL NEED

Dry piece of bark
2 large leaves
Tall stick
Small stick
Mud or paper clay
Moss
Acrylic paint
Scissors

This ship is ready to sail into its very own adventure!

1 Find a piece of bark that is a little bent.

2 Put some mud or paper clay in the center and front of your boat.

3 Make a pirate stick man.

Paint on his face and a stripy T-shirt, and use moss for his hair.

4 Push a long, straight stick into the mud for the mast.

Push the pirate into the mud at the front of the boat.

5 Cut some large leaves to make one large and one smaller sail.

Your pirate ship is ready to launch!

15

PEBBLE ART HIDE-AND-FIND

Paint your favorite bugs or animals and hide them for people to find later.

YOU WILL NEED

Smooth stones
Pencil
Pencil sharpener
Acrylic paint or markers
Box or bag to carry your stones in

1 Wash all of your stones and pebbles in warm, soapy water.

Leave them to dry.

2 Draw the outline of your bugs and animals in pencil on each of your chosen stones.

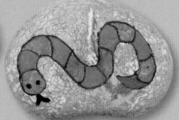

3 Carefully color in your drawings.

Leave them to dry.

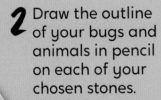

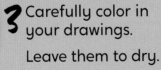

4 Store your stones in a bag or a box, ready for your next nature walk.

5 Hide your stones in secret places.

Will you remember where you left them?

Come back later, they might still be there!

BUILD A WOOD STACK

Make this small stack first, then build big!

YOU WILL NEED

Lots of straight sticks
Mud or super glue

1 Find a good place with lots of sticks and branches around.

2 Decide how big you want your stack to be. The bottom layer will be the longest.

3 You need four sticks the same length. Stack them like the photo above.

Leave a little space at each end. Use glue or mud to hold each layer in place.

4 Use sticks that are a little shorter for the next level. Keep going until it's as tall as you want it.

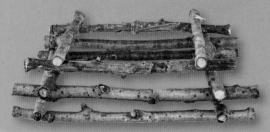

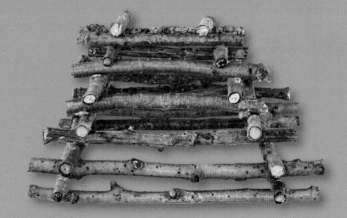

5 Use one tiny stick for the very top.

Now that you know how to build a small one, try building BIG!

You can build big stacks without using the mud, but it may not last as long.

COBWEB

Put some sticks around a tree trunk.
It makes a spooky spider web!

YOU WILL NEED

8 long sticks
8 medium sticks
8 small sticks

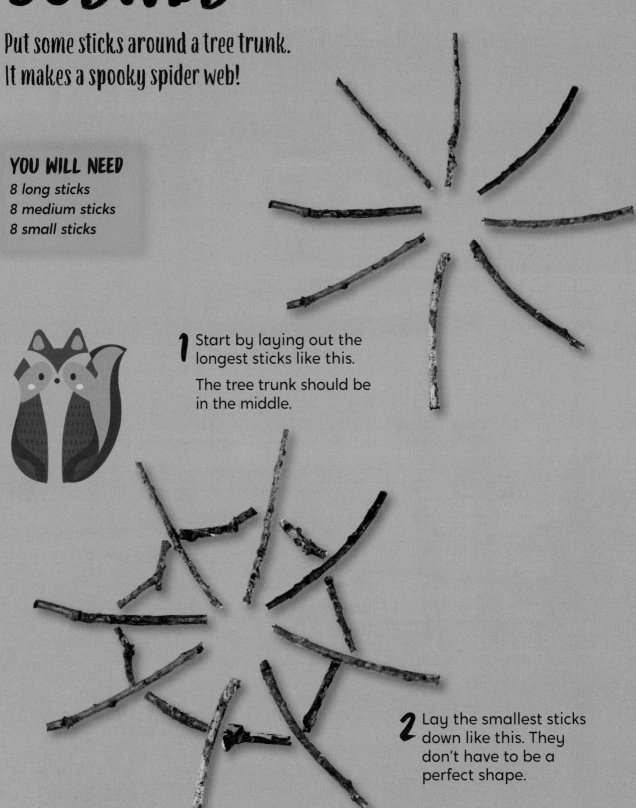

1 Start by laying out the longest sticks like this.

The tree trunk should be in the middle.

2 Lay the smallest sticks down like this. They don't have to be a perfect shape.

3 Lay the medium-size sticks down near the end of each long stick.

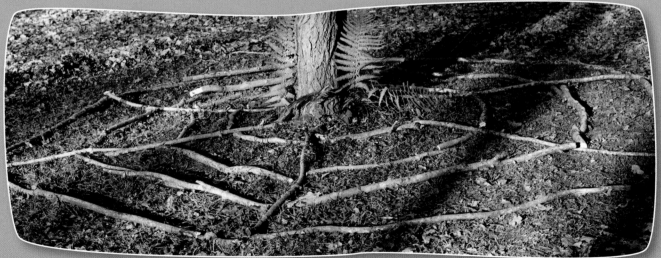

Now have fun making spooky webs wherever you go!

MINI CAMP

This little camp is super easy to make. Put in in your yard for your toys to play in!

YOU WILL NEED

3 strong sticks
Lots of thin sticks
Moss
Leaves
Vines or string

1 Find a flat surface on soft ground.

Put down some moss first.

2 Tie the three strong sticks together with vines or string.

Push the ends of the sticks into the moss.

3 Lay thin sticks on two sides of the strong sticks to make walls. The third side will be the door.

4 Cover the sticks with vines and leaves.

Your toys will have a blast in this nature camp!

BE CAREFUL OUTSIDE

It's always fun to play outside, but it's a good idea to . . .

. . . take water with you

. . . take a first aid kit for scratches and bug bites

. . . wear clothes and shoes for playing in the woods

. . . tell a grown-up where you are going

Safety First

Don't eat plants, and don't drink water you didn't bring with you.

If you are climbing, make sure you are with a grown-up.

Stay away from wild animals. They could be dangerous!

Be careful near water. It can be deeper than it looks.

Hungry Tomato®
An imprint of Lerner Publishing Group, Inc.
241 First Avenue North
Minneapolis, MN 55401 USA

For reading levels and more information, look up this title at www.lernerbooks.com.

Main body text set in Crossten.

Library of Congress Cataloging-in-Publication Data

ISBN 978-1-5415-5525-9 (lib. bdg.)
ISBN 978-1-5415-5526-6 (eb pdf)

Manufactured in the United States of America
1-45930-42824-4/10/2019

PICTURE CREDITS

(abbreviations: t = top; b = bottom; m = middle; l = left; r = right; bg = background)

Shutterstock: Brandy McKnight 18t; Hanet – all creatures, Ilyafs 12bg; Jitlada Panwiset 5br; openeyed 1 mr